50 Maple and Moose: A Taste of True North Recipes

By: Kelly Johnson

Table of Contents

- Maple-Glazed Moose Roast
- Bannock with Maple Butter
- Maple-Candied Salmon
- Moose Meat Chili
- Maple Baked Beans
- Cedar-Planked Maple Trout
- Maple Pecan Pie
- Wild Blueberry and Maple Muffins
- Smoked Moose Sausage
- Maple Whiskey BBQ Sauce
- Maple-Glazed Carrots
- Moose and Root Vegetable Stew
- Maple-Dijon Vinaigrette
- Maple Taffy on Snow
- Maple-Glazed Bacon
- Campfire Moose Burgers
- Maple Apple Crisp
- Roasted Maple Brussels Sprouts
- Maple Cranberry Sauce
- Wild Rice and Maple Pilaf
- Maple Cream Pie
- Grilled Moose Steaks with Maple Marinade
- Maple Glazed Donuts
- Maple Butter Tarts
- Maple and Nut Granola
- Moose Jerky with Maple Seasoning
- Maple Roasted Squash
- Maple Ice Cream
- Slow-Cooked Maple Pulled Moose
- Maple Roasted Nuts
- Maple Glazed Ham
- Maple Fudge
- Wild Berry and Maple Jam
- Maple Sweet Potato Mash
- Maple Roasted Chicken

- Maple-Spiced Hot Chocolate
- Campfire Moose Stew
- Maple Cinnamon Rolls
- Grilled Maple Pork Chops
- Maple and Apple Chutney
- Maple-Glazed Salmon Skewers
- Maple Pudding Cake
- Smoked Maple Trout Spread
- Maple-Walnut Shortbread
- Maple and Cranberry Glazed Duck
- Maple Chia Pudding
- Maple Balsamic Roasted Vegetables
- Maple Glazed Cornbread
- Maple and Herb Moose Roast
- Maple Scones with Wild Berries

Maple-Glazed Moose Roast

Ingredients

- 2 lb moose roast
- 1/4 cup maple syrup
- 2 tbsp Dijon mustard
- 2 tbsp soy sauce
- 2 cloves garlic, minced
- 1 tsp black pepper
- 1 tsp thyme

Instructions

1. Preheat oven to 325°F (165°C).
2. In a bowl, mix maple syrup, mustard, soy sauce, garlic, pepper, and thyme.
3. Brush glaze over the roast and place in a roasting pan.
4. Bake for 2-2.5 hours, basting occasionally, until tender.

Bannock with Maple Butter

Ingredients

- 2 cups flour
- 1 tbsp baking powder
- 1/2 tsp salt
- 1/4 cup butter, melted
- 3/4 cup water

Maple Butter

- 1/2 cup butter, softened
- 2 tbsp maple syrup

Instructions

1. Preheat oven to 375°F (190°C).
2. Mix flour, baking powder, and salt in a bowl.
3. Stir in melted butter and water to form a dough.
4. Shape into a round loaf and bake for 25-30 minutes.
5. Whisk softened butter with maple syrup and spread on warm bannock.

Maple-Candied Salmon

Ingredients

- 1 lb salmon fillet
- 1/4 cup maple syrup
- 2 tbsp soy sauce
- 1 tbsp Dijon mustard
- 1/2 tsp black pepper

Instructions

1. Preheat oven to 375°F (190°C).
2. Mix maple syrup, soy sauce, mustard, and pepper in a bowl.
3. Brush salmon with glaze and bake for 15-20 minutes.

Moose Meat Chili

Ingredients

- 1 lb ground moose meat
- 1 onion, chopped
- 2 cloves garlic, minced
- 1 can (14 oz) diced tomatoes
- 1 can (14 oz) kidney beans, drained
- 1 cup beef broth
- 2 tbsp tomato paste
- 1 tbsp chili powder
- 1 tsp cumin
- Salt and pepper to taste

Instructions

1. In a pot, brown moose meat with onion and garlic.
2. Add tomatoes, beans, broth, tomato paste, and spices.
3. Simmer for 45 minutes, stirring occasionally.

Maple Baked Beans

Ingredients

- 2 cups dried navy beans, soaked overnight
- 1/2 cup maple syrup
- 1/4 cup molasses
- 1/2 cup salt pork, diced
- 1 small onion, chopped
- 4 cups water
- 1/2 tsp mustard powder
- Salt and pepper to taste

Instructions

1. Preheat oven to 300°F (150°C).
2. In a baking dish, mix beans, syrup, molasses, salt pork, onion, water, mustard, salt, and pepper.
3. Cover and bake for 4-5 hours, stirring occasionally.

Cedar-Planked Maple Trout

Ingredients

- 1 whole trout, cleaned
- 1/4 cup maple syrup
- 1 tbsp soy sauce
- 1 clove garlic, minced
- 1 cedar plank, soaked in water

Instructions

1. Preheat grill to medium heat.
2. Mix maple syrup, soy sauce, and garlic, then brush over trout.
3. Place fish on soaked cedar plank and grill for 20-25 minutes.

Maple Pecan Pie

Ingredients

- 1 pie crust
- 3/4 cup maple syrup
- 1/2 cup brown sugar
- 3 eggs
- 1/4 cup butter, melted
- 1 cup pecans

Instructions

1. Preheat oven to 350°F (175°C).
2. Whisk maple syrup, brown sugar, eggs, and butter.
3. Stir in pecans and pour into the pie crust.
4. Bake for 40-45 minutes.

Wild Blueberry and Maple Muffins

Ingredients

- 1 1/2 cups flour
- 1/2 cup rolled oats
- 1/2 cup maple syrup
- 1/2 cup milk
- 1/4 cup butter, melted
- 1 egg
- 1 tsp vanilla extract
- 1 1/2 tsp baking powder
- 1/2 tsp baking soda
- 1/4 tsp salt
- 1 cup wild blueberries

Instructions

1. Preheat oven to 375°F (190°C). Line a muffin tin with liners.
2. In a bowl, mix flour, oats, baking powder, baking soda, and salt.
3. In another bowl, whisk maple syrup, milk, butter, egg, and vanilla.
4. Combine wet and dry ingredients, then fold in blueberries.
5. Divide into muffin cups and bake for 18-22 minutes.

Smoked Moose Sausage

Ingredients

- 2 lbs ground moose meat
- 1/2 lb pork fat, ground
- 2 tsp salt
- 1 tsp black pepper
- 1 tsp garlic powder
- 1/2 tsp smoked paprika
- 1/2 tsp thyme
- 1/4 cup cold water
- Natural sausage casings

Instructions

1. In a bowl, mix all ingredients thoroughly.
2. Stuff into sausage casings and twist into links.
3. Smoke at 200°F (95°C) for 2-3 hours until internal temperature reaches 160°F (70°C).

Maple Whiskey BBQ Sauce

Ingredients

- 1/2 cup maple syrup
- 1/4 cup whiskey
- 1 cup ketchup
- 2 tbsp apple cider vinegar
- 1 tbsp Dijon mustard
- 1 tbsp Worcestershire sauce
- 2 cloves garlic, minced
- 1/2 tsp smoked paprika
- 1/2 tsp black pepper

Instructions

1. In a saucepan, combine all ingredients.
2. Simmer for 15-20 minutes, stirring occasionally.
3. Let cool and store in a jar.

Maple-Glazed Carrots

Ingredients

- 4 cups carrots, sliced
- 2 tbsp butter
- 1/4 cup maple syrup
- 1/2 tsp cinnamon
- Salt and pepper to taste

Instructions

1. In a skillet, melt butter over medium heat.
2. Add carrots and cook until slightly tender.
3. Stir in maple syrup, cinnamon, salt, and pepper.
4. Cook for another 5 minutes until glazed.

Moose and Root Vegetable Stew

Ingredients

- 2 lbs moose meat, cubed
- 2 tbsp flour
- 2 tbsp butter
- 4 cups beef broth
- 2 potatoes, diced
- 2 carrots, sliced
- 1 parsnip, chopped
- 1 onion, chopped
- 2 cloves garlic, minced
- 1/2 tsp thyme
- 1/2 tsp black pepper
- Salt to taste

Instructions

1. Toss moose meat in flour.
2. Brown meat in butter in a pot.
3. Add broth, vegetables, garlic, thyme, and pepper.
4. Simmer for 2-3 hours until tender.

Maple-Dijon Vinaigrette

Ingredients

- 1/4 cup maple syrup
- 2 tbsp Dijon mustard
- 1/4 cup apple cider vinegar
- 1/2 cup olive oil
- Salt and pepper to taste

Instructions

1. Whisk all ingredients together in a bowl.
2. Drizzle over salad and serve.

Maple Taffy on Snow

Ingredients

- 1 cup maple syrup
- Fresh, clean snow

Instructions

1. Heat maple syrup in a saucepan to 235°F (112°C).
2. Pour in thin lines over packed snow.
3. Roll onto popsicle sticks and enjoy.

Maple-Glazed Bacon

Ingredients

- 12 slices bacon
- 1/4 cup maple syrup
- 1/2 tsp black pepper

Instructions

1. Preheat oven to 375°F (190°C).
2. Arrange bacon on a lined baking sheet.
3. Brush with maple syrup and sprinkle with black pepper.
4. Bake for 15-20 minutes until crispy.

Campfire Moose Burgers

Ingredients

- 1 lb ground moose meat
- 1/4 cup breadcrumbs
- 1 egg
- 1 tsp Worcestershire sauce
- 1/2 tsp garlic powder
- 1/2 tsp salt
- 1/4 tsp black pepper

Instructions

1. Mix all ingredients and form into patties.
2. Cook over a campfire or grill for 4-5 minutes per side.

Maple Apple Crisp

Ingredients

- 4 apples, sliced
- 1/2 cup maple syrup
- 1/2 cup rolled oats
- 1/4 cup flour
- 1/4 cup butter, melted
- 1/2 tsp cinnamon

Instructions

1. Preheat oven to 375°F (190°C).
2. Toss apples with maple syrup and place in a baking dish.
3. Mix oats, flour, butter, and cinnamon.
4. Sprinkle over apples and bake for 30 minutes.

Roasted Maple Brussels Sprouts

Ingredients

- 4 cups Brussels sprouts, halved
- 2 tbsp olive oil
- 1/4 cup maple syrup
- 1/2 tsp salt
- 1/4 tsp black pepper

Instructions

1. Preheat oven to 400°F (200°C).
2. Toss Brussels sprouts with olive oil, maple syrup, salt, and pepper.
3. Roast for 25-30 minutes until crispy.

Maple Cranberry Sauce

Ingredients

- 2 cups cranberries
- 1/2 cup maple syrup
- 1/2 cup orange juice
- 1/2 tsp cinnamon

Instructions

1. In a saucepan, combine cranberries, maple syrup, and orange juice.
2. Simmer until cranberries burst, about 10 minutes.
3. Stir in cinnamon and let cool.

Wild Rice and Maple Pilaf

Ingredients

- 1 cup wild rice
- 2 cups vegetable broth
- 1/4 cup maple syrup
- 1/4 cup pecans, toasted and chopped
- 1/4 cup dried cranberries
- 2 tbsp butter
- 1/2 tsp salt

Instructions

1. Rinse wild rice and cook in broth until tender, about 45 minutes.
2. Stir in maple syrup, butter, pecans, cranberries, and salt.
3. Let sit for 5 minutes before serving.

Maple Cream Pie

Ingredients

- 1 pie crust, pre-baked
- 2 cups milk
- 1/2 cup maple syrup
- 1/4 cup cornstarch
- 3 egg yolks
- 1/2 tsp vanilla extract
- 1/4 cup butter

Instructions

1. In a saucepan, heat milk and maple syrup.
2. Whisk cornstarch and egg yolks in a bowl. Slowly add hot milk.
3. Return mixture to the pan and cook until thickened.
4. Stir in vanilla and butter, then pour into pie crust. Chill before serving.

Grilled Moose Steaks with Maple Marinade

Ingredients

- 2 moose steaks
- 1/4 cup maple syrup
- 2 tbsp soy sauce
- 1 tbsp Dijon mustard
- 2 cloves garlic, minced
- 1/2 tsp black pepper

Instructions

1. Mix maple syrup, soy sauce, mustard, garlic, and pepper.
2. Marinate steaks for at least 2 hours.
3. Grill over medium heat for 5-6 minutes per side.

Maple Glazed Donuts

Ingredients

- 2 cups flour
- 1/2 cup sugar
- 1 tbsp baking powder
- 1/2 tsp salt
- 1/2 cup milk
- 2 eggs
- 1/4 cup butter, melted
- Oil for frying

Maple Glaze

- 1/2 cup maple syrup
- 1 cup powdered sugar

Instructions

1. Mix flour, sugar, baking powder, and salt.
2. Whisk in milk, eggs, and melted butter.
3. Roll out dough, cut into donuts, and fry at 350°F (175°C) until golden.
4. Whisk maple syrup and powdered sugar for glaze, then dip warm donuts.

Maple Butter Tarts

Ingredients

- 12 pre-made tart shells
- 1/2 cup maple syrup
- 1/2 cup brown sugar
- 1/4 cup butter, melted
- 1 egg
- 1/2 tsp vanilla extract

Instructions

1. Preheat oven to 375°F (190°C).
2. Whisk maple syrup, brown sugar, butter, egg, and vanilla.
3. Pour into tart shells and bake for 15-18 minutes.

Maple and Nut Granola

Ingredients

- 2 cups rolled oats
- 1/2 cup chopped almonds
- 1/2 cup chopped pecans
- 1/4 cup maple syrup
- 2 tbsp coconut oil, melted
- 1/2 tsp cinnamon

Instructions

1. Preheat oven to 325°F (165°C).
2. Mix oats, nuts, maple syrup, coconut oil, and cinnamon.
3. Spread on a baking sheet and bake for 20 minutes, stirring occasionally.

Moose Jerky with Maple Seasoning

Ingredients

- 1 lb moose meat, sliced thin
- 1/4 cup maple syrup
- 1/4 cup soy sauce
- 1 tsp black pepper
- 1/2 tsp garlic powder

Instructions

1. Marinate meat in maple syrup, soy sauce, pepper, and garlic powder overnight.
2. Dehydrate at 160°F (70°C) for 6-8 hours.

Maple Roasted Squash

Ingredients

- 1 butternut squash, peeled and cubed
- 2 tbsp maple syrup
- 1 tbsp olive oil
- 1/2 tsp cinnamon
- 1/2 tsp salt

Instructions

1. Preheat oven to 400°F (200°C).
2. Toss squash with maple syrup, oil, cinnamon, and salt.
3. Roast for 25-30 minutes.

Maple Ice Cream

Ingredients

- 2 cups heavy cream
- 1 cup milk
- 1/2 cup maple syrup
- 4 egg yolks

Instructions

1. Heat cream, milk, and maple syrup until warm.
2. Whisk egg yolks and slowly add hot mixture.
3. Return to heat and stir until thickened.
4. Chill and churn in an ice cream maker.

Slow-Cooked Maple Pulled Moose

Ingredients

- 2 lbs moose roast
- 1/2 cup maple syrup
- 1/2 cup beef broth
- 1/4 cup apple cider vinegar
- 1 tbsp Dijon mustard
- 2 cloves garlic, minced

Instructions

1. Place all ingredients in a slow cooker.
2. Cook on low for 6-8 hours until tender.
3. Shred with forks and serve.

Maple Roasted Nuts

Ingredients

- 2 cups mixed nuts (almonds, pecans, walnuts)
- 1/4 cup maple syrup
- 1 tbsp butter, melted
- 1/2 tsp cinnamon
- 1/4 tsp sea salt

Instructions

1. Preheat oven to 350°F (175°C).
2. Toss nuts with maple syrup, butter, cinnamon, and salt.
3. Spread on a baking sheet and roast for 12-15 minutes, stirring once.

Maple Glazed Ham

Ingredients

- 1 (6-8 lb) ham
- 1/2 cup maple syrup
- 1/4 cup Dijon mustard
- 1/4 cup brown sugar
- 1/2 tsp cloves

Instructions

1. Preheat oven to 325°F (165°C).
2. Score the ham and place in a roasting pan.
3. Mix maple syrup, mustard, brown sugar, and cloves. Brush over ham.
4. Bake for 2 hours, basting every 30 minutes.

Maple Fudge

Ingredients

- 2 cups maple syrup
- 1 cup heavy cream
- 2 tbsp butter
- 1/2 tsp vanilla extract

Instructions

1. In a saucepan, bring maple syrup and cream to a boil.
2. Simmer until mixture reaches 235°F (112°C).
3. Stir in butter and vanilla, then beat until thick.
4. Pour into a greased dish and let cool before cutting.

Wild Berry and Maple Jam

Ingredients

- 2 cups mixed wild berries
- 1/2 cup maple syrup
- 1 tbsp lemon juice
- 1 tsp pectin (optional)

Instructions

1. In a saucepan, combine berries, maple syrup, and lemon juice.
2. Simmer for 15-20 minutes, stirring frequently.
3. If using pectin, add in the last 5 minutes.
4. Let cool and store in jars.

Maple Sweet Potato Mash

Ingredients

- 3 large sweet potatoes, peeled and cubed
- 1/4 cup maple syrup
- 2 tbsp butter
- 1/2 tsp cinnamon
- Salt to taste

Instructions

1. Boil sweet potatoes until tender, then drain.
2. Mash with maple syrup, butter, cinnamon, and salt.

Maple Roasted Chicken

Ingredients

- 1 whole chicken
- 1/4 cup maple syrup
- 2 tbsp Dijon mustard
- 2 tbsp soy sauce
- 1 tsp thyme
- 1/2 tsp salt

Instructions

1. Preheat oven to 375°F (190°C).
2. Mix maple syrup, mustard, soy sauce, thyme, and salt.
3. Brush over chicken and roast for 1 hour, basting occasionally.

Maple-Spiced Hot Chocolate

Ingredients

- 2 cups milk
- 1/4 cup maple syrup
- 2 tbsp cocoa powder
- 1/2 tsp cinnamon
- 1/4 tsp nutmeg

Instructions

1. Heat milk, maple syrup, cocoa powder, cinnamon, and nutmeg in a saucepan.
2. Whisk until smooth and serve warm.

Campfire Moose Stew

Ingredients

- 2 lbs moose meat, cubed
- 4 cups beef broth
- 2 potatoes, diced
- 2 carrots, sliced
- 1 onion, chopped
- 2 cloves garlic, minced
- 1/2 tsp thyme
- 1/2 tsp black pepper
- Salt to taste

Instructions

1. In a pot over a campfire, brown moose meat.
2. Add broth, vegetables, garlic, thyme, pepper, and salt.
3. Simmer for 2-3 hours until tender.

Maple Cinnamon Rolls

Ingredients

- 2 1/2 cups flour
- 1/4 cup sugar
- 1 tbsp baking powder
- 1/2 tsp salt
- 1/2 cup milk
- 1/4 cup butter, melted
- 1/4 cup maple syrup

Instructions

1. Preheat oven to 375°F (190°C).
2. Mix flour, sugar, baking powder, and salt.
3. Stir in milk and melted butter to form dough.
4. Roll out, brush with maple syrup, and roll up.
5. Cut into slices and bake for 15-18 minutes.

Grilled Maple Pork Chops

Ingredients

- 4 pork chops
- 1/4 cup maple syrup
- 2 tbsp soy sauce
- 1 tbsp Dijon mustard
- 1/2 tsp black pepper

Instructions

1. Mix maple syrup, soy sauce, mustard, and black pepper.
2. Marinate pork chops for at least 1 hour.
3. Grill over medium heat for 4-5 minutes per side.

Maple and Apple Chutney

Ingredients

- 2 apples, peeled and diced
- 1/2 cup maple syrup
- 1/4 cup apple cider vinegar
- 1/2 cup onion, chopped
- 1/4 cup raisins
- 1/2 tsp cinnamon
- 1/4 tsp nutmeg
- 1/4 tsp salt

Instructions

1. In a saucepan, combine all ingredients.
2. Bring to a boil, then reduce heat and simmer for 25-30 minutes, stirring occasionally.
3. Let cool before storing in jars.

Maple-Glazed Salmon Skewers

Ingredients

- 1 lb salmon, cut into cubes
- 1/4 cup maple syrup
- 2 tbsp soy sauce
- 1 tbsp Dijon mustard
- 1 tsp garlic, minced
- 1/2 tsp black pepper
- Wooden skewers (soaked in water)

Instructions

1. In a bowl, mix maple syrup, soy sauce, mustard, garlic, and pepper.
2. Marinate salmon cubes for 30 minutes.
3. Thread onto skewers and grill over medium heat for 3-4 minutes per side.

Maple Pudding Cake

Ingredients

- 1 cup flour
- 1 tsp baking powder
- 1/4 tsp salt
- 1/2 cup milk
- 1/4 cup butter, melted
- 1/4 cup sugar
- 1 tsp vanilla extract
- 1 cup maple syrup
- 1 cup hot water

Instructions

1. Preheat oven to 350°F (175°C). Grease a baking dish.
2. In a bowl, mix flour, baking powder, salt, milk, butter, sugar, and vanilla.
3. Spread batter into the baking dish.
4. In a saucepan, heat maple syrup and hot water. Pour over batter.
5. Bake for 35 minutes until golden and bubbly.

Smoked Maple Trout Spread

Ingredients

- 1 cup smoked trout, flaked
- 2 tbsp maple syrup
- 4 oz cream cheese
- 1 tbsp lemon juice
- 1 tbsp chopped chives
- 1/2 tsp black pepper

Instructions

1. In a bowl, mix smoked trout, maple syrup, cream cheese, lemon juice, chives, and pepper.
2. Blend until smooth and chill before serving.

Maple-Walnut Shortbread

Ingredients

- 1 cup butter, softened
- 1/2 cup maple syrup
- 2 cups all-purpose flour
- 1/2 cup walnuts, chopped
- 1/4 tsp salt

Instructions

1. Preheat oven to 325°F (165°C).
2. Cream butter and maple syrup together.
3. Add flour, walnuts, and salt, mixing until dough forms.
4. Roll out and cut into shapes or press into a pan.
5. Bake for 20-25 minutes until golden.

Maple and Cranberry Glazed Duck

Ingredients

- 2 duck breasts
- 1/4 cup maple syrup
- 1/4 cup cranberry juice
- 1 tbsp Dijon mustard
- 1 tsp balsamic vinegar
- 1/2 tsp salt
- 1/2 tsp black pepper

Instructions

1. Preheat oven to 375°F (190°C).
2. Score duck skin and season with salt and pepper.
3. Sear duck breasts skin-side down for 5 minutes, then transfer to the oven for 10 minutes.
4. In a saucepan, heat maple syrup, cranberry juice, mustard, and vinegar until thickened.
5. Brush glaze over duck before serving.

Maple Chia Pudding

Ingredients

- 1/2 cup chia seeds
- 2 cups milk or almond milk
- 1/4 cup maple syrup
- 1 tsp vanilla extract

Instructions

1. In a bowl, mix chia seeds, milk, maple syrup, and vanilla.
2. Stir well and refrigerate for at least 4 hours, stirring occasionally.
3. Serve chilled with berries or nuts.

Maple Balsamic Roasted Vegetables

Ingredients

- 2 cups mixed vegetables (carrots, Brussels sprouts, sweet potatoes)
- 2 tbsp maple syrup
- 1 tbsp balsamic vinegar
- 2 tbsp olive oil
- 1/2 tsp salt
- 1/2 tsp black pepper

Instructions

1. Preheat oven to 400°F (200°C).
2. Toss vegetables with maple syrup, balsamic vinegar, olive oil, salt, and pepper.
3. Spread on a baking sheet and roast for 25-30 minutes, stirring once.

Maple Glazed Cornbread

Ingredients

- 1 cup cornmeal
- 1 cup flour
- 1 tbsp baking powder
- 1/2 tsp salt
- 1/2 cup milk
- 1/4 cup maple syrup
- 1/4 cup butter, melted
- 2 eggs

Instructions

1. Preheat oven to 375°F (190°C).
2. Mix dry ingredients in one bowl and wet ingredients in another.
3. Combine both mixtures and stir until smooth.
4. Pour into a greased baking dish and bake for 25-30 minutes.

Maple and Herb Moose Roast

Ingredients

- 2 lb moose roast
- 1/4 cup maple syrup
- 2 tbsp olive oil
- 1 tbsp Dijon mustard
- 2 cloves garlic, minced
- 1 tsp thyme
- 1 tsp rosemary
- Salt and pepper to taste

Instructions

1. Preheat oven to 325°F (165°C).
2. Rub moose roast with olive oil, maple syrup, mustard, garlic, thyme, rosemary, salt, and pepper.
3. Place in a roasting pan and cook for 2-2.5 hours, basting occasionally.

Maple Scones with Wild Berries

Ingredients

- 2 cups flour
- 1 tbsp baking powder
- 1/2 tsp salt
- 1/4 cup butter, cold and cubed
- 1/4 cup maple syrup
- 1/2 cup milk
- 1/2 cup wild berries

Instructions

1. Preheat oven to 375°F (190°C).
2. Mix flour, baking powder, and salt. Cut in butter until crumbly.
3. Stir in maple syrup, milk, and berries until combined.
4. Shape into a circle, cut into wedges, and bake for 18-20 minutes.

www.ingramcontent.com/pod-product-compliance
Lightning Source LLC
LaVergne TN
LVHW081341060526
838201LV00055B/2788